THE WATER WE SWIM IN

POEMS

Christian Aldana

Sampaguita
Press

The Water We Swim In
Published by Sampaguita Press
Sampaguita Press LLC
P.O. Box 731305
San Jose, CA 95173

www.SampaguitaPress.com

Book design by Sampaguita Press
Cover artwork by Cori Nakamura Lin

ISBN 979-8-9857712-6-8 (paperback)
ISBN 979-8-9857712-7-5 (ebook)

Further Praise for
THE WATER WE SWIM IN

"In Christian Aldana's *The Water We Swim In*, the details of our everyday lives transform into symbols of possibility. Text messages become incantations and lists become invocations. These formally inventive poems function not only as protest (against violence, colonialism, abuse) but also as praise to the sacred power of community: the Filipinx *we* and queer *we* and radical *we* that in these pages grieves and loves and rages and sings together. In this spiritual and yet deeply embodied book, Aldana both reimagines the world we live in and builds the one worth waiting for. We are lucky to be invited."

—**JAMI NAKAMURA LIN**, author of *The Night Parade*

"Christian Aldana's *The Water We Swim In* pilots us through the waters of the past few years, waters that are murky with the COVID pandemic, endless violence against marginalized bodies, and profound grief. With a complex voice—playful humor thorned with grief—Aldana leads us through the water to those shards of sunlight that slice through the water's surface. Even when overwhelmed with this world's tragedies, Aldana 'found a way to become.'"

—**TAYLOR BYAS**, author of *Bloodwarm* and *Shutter*

"*The Water We Swim In* is a raucous baptism of queer brown joy, calamansi raunch, and divine abolitionist, anticolonial, collective power. Mga kasama, Aldana reminds us that 'our life is a truth we have fought for, / there is nothing more precious than you.' Whether we are wiping teargas from our eyes or searching for ourselves and our people at the bookstore, Aldana's ferocious voice and tender attention to craft is here to guide us—and I do mean, us. Aldana's vision for kami is a call to action, hope distilled."

—**RACHELLE CRUZ**, author of *God's Will for Monsters*

"There is risk in *The Water We Swim In*, and a profoundly attentive poetics of appreciation. In sharp work that moves with emotional and formal agility, the voices talk dangerous, fighting, dancing, and Christian Aldana—in listening with them—invokes the type of gentleness towards which the poems reach. Oof, let me tell you, the poems reach. Unabashedly (praise be). Committed to multiple iterations of love we need right now. Which is to say, ongoing and beyond. Here is one of Aldana's imperatives: 'your kanta should conjure an altar / overflowing with offerings.' And *The Water We Swim In* does."

—**HARI ALLURI**, author of *The Flayed City* and *Our Echo of Sudden Mercy*

"*The Water We Swim In* is a tome of protection spells and rituals for self, family, and community—a manifesto of deeply embodied hope. This collection is at once dreamy and a fighter, its presence abundant in the voices it praises, inviting us to sit still in reflection then break out into dance. Aldana extends a brave hand toward the reader, leading them with deep intention and compassion through raucous Filipino Martial Arts practice and quiet moments cleaning pepper spray off skin. A spectacular, long-awaited debut."

—**CZAERRA GALICINAO UCOL**, Programs & Communications Director of Luya Poetry; author of *Pisces Urges*

"Christian Aldana's *The Water We Swim In* is a punch to the gut and a tender hug all at the same time. Wading through the seas of white supremacy, police brutality, colonialism, and violent masculinity, Aldana's poetry is a life raft of revolutionary love and radical joy. This cinematic collection of Filipinx warrior poetry settles in the body and shifts the heart—nothing is the same after *The Water We Swim In*."

—**BUTCH SCHWARZKOPF**, author of *Pagong Cannot Climb Trees* for my kasamas, for my friends

      who have made this city feel like home —

you have cared for me, politicized me, challenged me,

      danced with me, believed in me, and shown me

         that a better world is possible

            you are building it right now

salamat kaayo

Note to the Reader & Content Warning

Dear Reader,

This collection of poems deals with themes of grief, police brutality, racism, and assault. There are poems in this book about sex, about gender and gender roles, about queerness, about family. These poems delve into our shared history as a Filipino diaspora, so these poems address colonization, imperialism, militarism, war, migration, labor pipelines, Catholicism, the pandemic.

These poems are also full of hope, joy, and radical imagination.

I am so honored that you are reading this work, and I invite you to pause, to skip poems, to read in whatever order you need to in order to care for yourself.

Contents

Crafting Our Safety Plan: A Foreword

I first encountered Christian Aldana's revolutionary poetry and poetics through The Digital Sala. In April 2020, as this global health emergency continued to escalate, as freedom struggles across the globe continued to remind us of radical possibility, as our differential vulnerabilities to the criminal accumulation of capital were laid bare, as racist state terror proceeded to do what racist state terror does to our minds and bodies, writers and workers across various diasporas—in this instance, the Filipino diaspora—sought care and community. And thus emerged The Digital Sala, against cultural gatekeeping, against the ruse of prestige, against policing, against borders, against violence, for our communities, for our peoples. In the spirit of collaboration, experimentation, radical openness, and deep and genuine relationship-building, The Digital Sala supported the literary magazine *Marías at Sampaguitas* in co-hosting an open mic. Poet after poet, this open mic revealed with a tender and playful clarity the fire and multitude of contemporary Filipino diasporic poetry. When Aldana, clearly a seasoned and confident performer, showed up on screen, she/they introduced herself/their self, represented Chicago, and said, "I'm bringing that queer disaster energy." I could not help but trace this 'queer disaster energy' to Audre Lorde's radical erotics in "Movement Song" in which the speaker reminds us to "not remember [them] as disaster / nor as the keeper of secrets" (88). For me, Lorde's critical humility makes possible the 'queer disaster energy' of Aldana's poetics.

While the scenes and cartographies of Aldana's poems evoke the vastness of transnational solidarity, Aldana's poetics play in an abundance generated through a rigorously queer intimacy. In these troubled waters, we find respite, real rest, real dreaming, in the quiet acts of "[pressing] down with the / knife to ease the [garlic] clove out of its skin" (25). In these troubled waters, we are returned to the slow and quiet worry for our ancestors, our youth, our futures. A kind of water themselves, the poems in this remarkable debut take shape in sestina, pantoum, cento, free verse, performance. The 'queer disaster energy' of Aldana's poetics takes on a form and genre of expanse, the oceanic, the forever flowing river, the capaciousness of "what it's like to be queer" and the "want to live, and live, and live" (59).

In *The Water We Swim In*, we encounter queer Filipina poet, performer, abolitionist, organizer, cultural worker, mentor, kasama, lover, martial arts practitioner, daughter, mother maybe, 'queer disaster energy' in the streets, at the park, in the kitchen, in and of and for the water. This is "poetry for mutual aid poetry for birthdays poetry for grieving" (12). In this poetry, the police will never ever keep us safe, only "we [will] keep us safe" (16). In this poetry, we witness the courage of a queer erotics of grief, "a grieving in diaspora" (28). In "Uses of the Erotic," Lorde describes "the erotic [as] a measure between the beginnings of our sense of self and the chaos of our strongest feelings" (54). The speaker(s) of Aldana's poems only know her/their body/bodies as "a body during the sharp disaster of fresh, / ripened grief" (40); she/they know that her/their body is "the loudest despedida in the barangay" (58); she/they know that "grief gives shape to [their] body / like nothing else" (55). And in this book, the water that we swim in is not solely the troublesome waters of white supremacy, colonialism, and/or racial capitalism. These poems teach us to river our ways back to each other. These poems remind us that we are "a river, a rush, a dream" (45). These waters are full of the dialectics of struggle—the water we swim in, the we water we bend, the water we are.

In "Pantoum for 2032", Aldana shares as an epigraph a brief excerpt from "A Comrade is as Precious as a Rice Seedling" by Mila D. Aguilar, Filipina poet, essayist, documentary filmmaker, former political prisoner and survivor of the dehumanizing and murderous

Marcos dictatorship. It should be noted that it was Audre Lorde and Kitchen Table: Women of Color Press that, in an act of solidarity, published Aguilar's book. Meditating on this gesture, I cannot help but think of Aldana the poet and cultural worker as also the founder of the radical, queer, Chicago-based literary organization Luya, as also the youth mentor and community organizer. Aldana walks this world versed in the teachings of revolutionaries like Aguilar, Lorde, and Grace Lee Boggs. Thus, it is no wonder that these poetics are a community poetics. These poetics emerge through a fluency in social struggle. It is no wonder, then, that the speaker in "Pantoum for 2032" affirms that "we are millions enough for the thunder" (46).

In the middle of reading *The Water We Swim In*, I found myself studying a brief interview with Mila D. Aguilar. In the interview, Aguilar reflects on going underground, being imprisoned, and being brutalized. Even though I have been teaching and learning from Aguilar's work for a little over two decades, I had never heard Aguilar's voice until I encountered this interview. I have rehearsed, interpreted, sampled, and shared widely "The People's Poem." There is so much stillness in this poem, so much distillation, so much desire. The line that closes the first stanza is a gentle and soft violence. After describing the delicateness of a "thin, worn string" whose "growing knot itself / becomes the breaking point," the speaker reveals rather softly: "Then something snaps forever" (11). It is within this snap, the quiet sound of very thin threads abruptly torn apart, the dialectical struggle between two different forms of power—peoples' power and the oppressor's power, that I find the promise of a growing revolutionary Filipino poetics. It is within this snap, a forever, that I read Christian Aldana's *The Water We Swim In*. Aldana writes and struggles in the tradition of Mila D. Aguilar's revolutionary poetics, for there is something soft, quiet, dignified, and necessarily rageful about how both Aguilar's and Aldana's poetics move us, lift us, river us. At the end of the interview with Aguilar, I hear the quiet wisdom of revolution as she reminds us: "Never give up democracy. Kasi once you give it up, patay tayong lahat." I am humbled by the fact that the publication of Christian Aldana's *The Water We Swim In* by the people-of-color-led Sampaguita Press arrives 39 years after Kitchen Table: Women of Color Press published *A Comrade is as Precious as a Rice Seedling*. I invite us all to meditate on what our literary ancestors have made possible for us as poets, as readers, as fighters. From book to book, from generation to generation, we are reminded to never give up, that we have each other. In Aldana's words, "there will always be more of us / until there's none of them" (19). Isulong!

This book is a workshop in revolutionary care: "how many tender words can [we] say without cost?" (63) This book helps us believe that "we belong here, and everywhere" (64). This book is for you, Kasama. This book is for you, Compa. This book is for you, Comrade. This book is for us, tayo, tayong lahat. Trust: Christian Aldana's *The Water We Swim In* is crafting our safety plan.

Makibaka! Huwag matakot!

Jason Magabo Perez
San Diego, California
April 2023

Works Cited

Aguilar, Mila D. "The People's Poem." *A Comrade is as Precious as a Rice Seedling*. Kitchen Table: Women of Color Press, 1984.

Lorde, Audre. "Movement Song." *The Collected Poems of Audre Lorde*. Norton, 1997, pp. 88-89.

Lorde, Audre. "Uses of the Erotic: The Erotic as Power." *Sister Outsider: Essays and Speeches*. Crossing Press, 1987, 2007, pp. 53-69.

THE WATER
WE SWIM IN

What Happened in 2020, an inventory of self

I hate work but   damn
a new job with benefits where I feel   respected? who would have thought
czaerra and I   would build something   that feels like family
police beat me up beat us all up   over a damn
statue   at least now I know how to deal with pepper spray   new skills
like how to   jail support phone zap plan direct action   be safe at direct
action   civil disobedience
said no to   pigs and   romances that did not serve me
sex as the world ends   start a lover   end another   a few times   safely
didn't get the virus   knock on wood   pray on a nose swab
abolition means   everything abolition is   difficult abolition needs
so much hope as much as we are critical
unlearn/ing/ed capitalism and   relearn/ing/ed that deep personal
relationships make
or break movements
I don't like organizing   with people who aren't committed
to something outside   the belly of the beast
I don't like organizing   with people who aren't committed
to their own   people   culture who aren't learning from their history
of migration colonization   imperialism
performed poetry to my empty bedroom   but so many zoom rooms
depaul lavender grad   interaction fundraiser   luyaluyaluya   bulosan center
university of minnesota
poetry for mutual aid poetry for birthdays poetry for grieving
my poetry idol bjr   asked me to perform with her   and it's fine if I never
do anything else after that I'm happy
taught workshops   went to workshops   planned workshops
got published   got rejected   wrote edited sent hoped let go
got nominated   what's a pushcart?   they still use snail mail?
expanded   awestruck   transnational filipinx poet kaleidoscope

nasaan ang sala?   kahit saan kase digital!

what's an MFA?   grad   school? for poems?   I'm still scared

but at least I have people to look up to now like jason and rachelle and hari

to my sibs   i sent memes   i broke down   broke open

Ate is human too   with her bad brain   and they still love me even when i

am not useful

i learned to drive   i went outside   i bought a wok   weed

glass pipes to smoke with   pink rolling papers   an altar tray

really it's a rolling tray   but with moon phases

gained weight   and still have a nice ass

bitch

"Hope is a discipline."
—Mariame Kaba

"They got evil plans in the Devil's hands
but I don't pray 'cause I organize.
They got new ways to impose strength
but I teach mine how to mobilize."
—Rocky Rivera, "Us"

"THOSE WHO COME FROM ISLANDS KNOW ME AS THE
LONGING—FLUID TO A GENDER—HARANA TO YOUR
ORIGIN: I'M SUNG—CHORUS OF BANGKA JOURNEY TO
BECOME, INCANTATION TO BEGIN—"
—Hari Alluri, "Seeking Union + Returning: Ang tubig ay buhay"

my student asks me what she should bring to the protest

tells me she has cash, you know,

               in case, and

                         should she bring her phone?

she's read the infographics too

     and here we are, mouthing off on our smartphones

     about surveillance.

I rattle

     off the list from memory:

     wear black, comfortable shoes in case ~~we have to run~~, layers

     for weather,

     water bottle in case she gets thirsty

                     ~~pepper sprayed~~

     phone, charging bank, a sign

~~should I tell her goggles, helmet, umbrella?~~

she says,

         I know someone who looks like Adam.

I ask the questions I'm supposed to about parents and friends and rides to and from.

I tell her our safety plan:

        the meeting point,

            the friends who will be with us,

                  how long we will stay,

           what we mean when we say *escalate*,

        what we plan to do if it *escalates*,

    how we make it home ~~when it escalates~~.

I say,

     we keep us safe.

but what's safe ~~when the pigs have their gun on you?~~

I say,

     I used to teach kids who looked like Adam.

STOP TELLING ME POLICE WILL KEEP US SAFE

asian people are dying and there are no answers; i heard ten rounds in my alleyway last week; someone shot a kid in front of an elementary school in albany park; maybe i shouldn't take transit as often as i do; i wish i could afford a car; i'm sick of people telling me that we should go to the police when we're hurt, why should we run to something that hurts us; how many women like me have been laughed out of a police station; how many sex workers in asia have they assaulted; white men have been preying on me since i was twelve and i'm sick; men go to southeast asia on their little trips and think we only exist to serve them

Pepper spray

I lean back into the stream of water
to make sure the chemicals don't flow back into my eyes
the internet said to wash yourself with dish soap
said you might have to wash several times
said to wash your protest clothes separately
said to soak your clothes before washing them

I want to soak my brain in something to dissolve my fear
I keep thinking about the raised baton as he walked towards me
me, on the ground and flinching
keep thinking about how he marched straight past
keep thinking about who he beat instead
who had to make a pit stop at the ER before going home tonight
or maybe didn't make it home at all
had to sit in a jail cell, skin burning
while their lungs struggle to draw breath

everytime my hair moves I smell it again
I keep my breaths shallow, careful
keep scrubbing slowly, gently
keep saying I fell but really we were pushed
keep saying I tripped but really we were thrown
downplay my bruises to get through
they play up the *riot* on the news
I keep scrubbing, gently, avoiding my bruises
I wash myself like a small child scared of bathtime
washing my forehead is the hardest part
I have to twist myself so the water flows off my temples
just like I had to twist myself out the way of their fists

I keep thinking about how next time, we'll twist faster
we'll duck lower, we'll wear long sleeves
next time, we'll have helmets, and goggles, and shields too
I keep thinking about how there will always be a next time
there will always be more of us
until there's none of them.

Texting

sorry I missed this
sorry, there are still 26 unread messages on my phone

> *how have you been?*
>> *how are you staying grounded in this time?*
> how are you keeping all the pieces of yourself
>> from disintegrating?

>>>> *no worries, there's a lot going on*
>>> *right now,*

do you know how
> to keep yourself tightly   coiled, have I missed something?
>> haveimissedsomething

>> *my head and my heart are*   *everywhere, lol*
>>> *it's ok*

it's ok

>>> *text me when you get home?*

>>>>>> *i*   *will*   *:)*

i want someone to know I'm still here
> i have 2̶6̶, 8̶4̶, 9̶9̶, 110 unread messages
but I answered   yours

just checking in
i made it home safe
> *how have you been?*
i made it home safe

24

what are you up to?

i made it home safe

            how are you feeling?

i made it home safe

              are you ok?

i made it home safe

are

                you

                        ok?

4:00AM in Chicago

is 5:00PM in Manila, so my mother must have started
making dinner by now. I'm not jealous
of how good that meal must be, of the alchemy

she turns on to the plate. I'm fine
with ice cream for dinner, or spiteful
pieces of toast from the only loaf left in the Jewel

Osco bread aisle. I really should call my mother, after
all I am awake at such a convenient time
difference, but what would I say after

the click, the dial? The days blur
together, tick, tick, tick into an endless
carousel tock of time. I order

food when I am not hungry, should I tell
her that binge eating and not eating
come from the same dying

place, that all my taste buds are
desperate to drown in flavor
in case the virus comes for them. I sleep

at 4:00AM to make up for being home
at reasonable hours, you know, mum
I'm fine.

Recipe cards

How long does the scent of garlic cling? Later, when my lover puts my fingers in his steaming mouth, will they still carry the kitchen with them?

They say the proof is in the pudding, so I make it. The proof is in the first bite, the last swallow, the pretty yellow gold of the custard that makes its graceful chassé down your chin.

I am trying to remember my father praising my mother for something other than her cooking. My mother is a goddess until the plates are clean.

I make pasta to apologize. According to the notes from my mother, carbonara must be made carefully, otherwise you end up with scrambled eggs. So my eggs are perfect. My lover swallows and smiles, and smiles and swallows, and I trade his cold shoulder for a warm mouth. I watch him go back for seconds and never question that I am the one to blame.

Domesticity looks good on me, slaps my ass, pulls on my taut nipples, leads me to the bedroom by the chef's knife.

Everything I make is delicious, I polish off the praise. How I love to say thank you, thank you.

I learn to make biko. And ragu. And chickpea curry. I learn to make sinigang from scratch, from the lemons I have, I make do. I learn to make the ginger sing against the garlic cloves I crush with the flat of the knife. I make red curries, kimchi stews, and bone broth soups. I roll out my own pie crust and pack it with all the warmth I can coax out of an apple. I learn to be a goddess, a trophy, a compensation for my round form, my loud mouth.

My mother taught me to slice off the end of the clove first.

I learn to arch my back and say *please*. I learn not to answer, because he doesn't teach me to ask. I consider learning how to bake bread, how to make an onion galette, how to prepare oxtail, how to ferment my own tea, how to anticipate a need.

My mother taught me to press down with the knife to ease the clove out of its skin.

Reading Audre Lorde in the kitchen, 3 days before you decided to leave me

It's been a week and I still love you.
The love-bites you left on my right breast

still there, yellowing softly like a handful of leaves
in decay. I feel my outline slowly dissipating without

your mouth to steady it. I knew better
where I was going when you held my hands

behind my back: kept me helpless, focused. Slipped out
of my feminist finery and into roleplay, I sizzle

aromatics in the kitchen. Your spice rack wheezes
at me, I've accepted that sons rarely learn

to cook in your culture. You read to me about how to raise a man.
You are so pleased to tell me what you've learned.

I have already raised so many boys but in our domestic scene
I am a patient woman. A straight woman.

Military boys break so easily from the blunt force
of their fathers. *Men who are afraid to feel*

must keep women around to do their feeling for them—
You don't want to be like him, but where did you learn

to treat me like this—*dismissing us for the same*
supposedly "inferior" capacity to feel deeply.

My empty womb clenches
around your words, I am thankful

for the distraction of the stove. It is just biology
at work but I run full tilt into the fantasy,

cast you as the father, your son on my hip,
with my eyes and your cowlick.

In your grin I see the dream: arch me
over this counter, make a mother out of me.

First year death anniversary

grieving in diaspora is the priest getting disconnected
from the video call mid-prayer
the rainfall in your homeland too heavy
for the internet to bear

the responsorial psalm doubled
in a discordant echo, as your mourning
lags through time zones, prayer
trembling through your speakers

powerpoint songs replace the choir
you lip-sync karaoke-style devotions
in your swivel chair, while the skies
shatter over Cebu

every sibling in a separate
cell, mouthing unfamiliar gospels,
out-of-sync videos splicing your grief
across computer screens

in Chicago, the morose snow gusts
weakly out of season, the priest
reminds you, thirteen hours in the future,
it is the fifth Sunday of lent in the Philippines

shouldn't you all be together, umbrellas jostling
in the cemetery, sweat collecting under collars
the smell of grease from someone's memorial feast
scenting the air, a family resemblance in your smiles

you weep-from-home at your work desk
holding a rosary to play-act religion
you curse America, Duterte, the pandemic
over every wooden bead

2032

All my friends can't hang anymore,
can't keep their eyes open past 10:00PM. We wake
up in time to catch the tail end of the sunrise, we are all morning
people now. We stopped sleeping
       with one eye open.

Of course, the kids don't even say "hang" anymore,
they have new incantations to enchant
their joy, their lexicon is a set of unknown
spells. It's so magical to be outdated
       and alive.

All my friends write sweet poems now,
lollipop stanzas. They pull sugar
through all the syllables, a rush
of gratitude in their smiles. How lucky
we are with our front yards, and our gardens teeming
with children and summer fruits. How opulent
to know peace, and to never have to ask
       if everyone made it home safe.

STOP TELLING ME POLICE WILL KEEP US SAFE

for my Filipino Martial Arts family, after our teacher Crystle Dino

i laugh at the cat-shaped knuckle duster,
small enough to daisy-chain to my keyring,
ears filed to menacing points: i want to be sharp
enough on my own.

i spend so much time lying
about boyfriends i don't have, avoiding
the invitation to the hotel room, the bar,
the back of the room, the sidewalk
i say everything except *no*
because they are leaning too close
they are walking to my rhythm
they are chasing a fantasy, a high, a prize
they are following me, you, us.

i'm trying to be good
at being alone, but they love you
by yourself

in the park, armed with bamboo sticks,
we put a hand to our third eyes
          the other to our hearts, a sign of respect
before we fight: we fly
over the elastic ground, sticks whistling
before crashing against each other like waves
          who will keep us safe?
not this country, not the cops, only us,
          our own wit, our own sweat, our own blood

when the sun goes down
you should sit in the front car of the red line
          one time i forgot
he pleaded with me, *just one hug*
a train car full of lonely
men, minding their business not minding
me, shrinking, shaking, apologizing
for not accommodating, trying
not to make any sudden moves

the knuckle duster is pink and i don't buy it
i imagine hooking my fingers through its eyes
grinning cat-face resting in my too-small palm
i don't know the first thing about fighting, so
what good would a weapon do?

in the park, we learn the truth of our movements,
we imagine ourselves with blades:
diagonal strikes to split a man open
from shoulder to waist, strike
from below to disembowel,
a circular strike from above
to sever the head from the neck.

Men[1] fear[2] me but can't stop[3] telling me[4] their secrets[5]

---

[1] Plaintive lambs come to the slaughter willingly. They lean close in dark places, I could reach out and trace their skulls. Hunger hollows their eyes, need pulsing, brows arch as they bleat their deepest remorses.

[2] This hallowed meeting ground. My finest pout perched on a barstool, under the pretense of what they are too scared to ask for: a devouring. Their starved hands gesture toward heaven, unpromised, unsullied–they are careful to gut themselves without drawing blood.

[3] Some of them want to touch me first, ready to be shorn before spilling themselves at my feet. Others prefer to anticipate sin, glut themselves on almosts: the brush of a finger on glass, knees, palms, a hip.

[4] They want me to know. They are *grateful, sorry, saved.*

[5] I catch their urgent wishes in my cupped hands, cradle them against my blade.

Call Center

when the customer intoned
cinnamon skin and dark hair drives me crazy
I remembered to smile through the microphone tried to push
the corners of my mouth into the internet so he'd hear
all my little teeth clack into position grinning
like a fantasy

haven't I learned the right way
to set the mood to pull myself from the bottom
of man's delusions with every hair in place
filipina of your daydreams
little mynah bird to mirror affectations

all our women fold together
little paper doll chains for him
pleasant in expression as he regales
me with his string of romances
with women who look like me

I don't have room for this shit anymore
if I was selling you couldn't buy
I'd bleed you dry and wouldn't be sorry
let the pennies echo in your little skull

I unfuck myself from a set of desperate eyes
fly through your ready armed loneliness
I'm up I'm up I'm sky you're groundbelly
little creature slithering in the dirt leave me
I got time enough to kill

I got enough of me to fill the space up
your little cuts can't steal my size fight
me I'm better I've learned I'm not waiting
to be a hospitable womb I'm wicked I'm
something to kneel to you're worthless

Half-Past King Philip

I never expect to find us in the bookstore. I try anyway. I check for us in the non-fiction, because I know our history is real. I think I might find my people in the poetry section. It's poetic how a populace can go on living through every new oppressive presidency. I run my fingers along every shelf. I linger on every Spanish author.

Hernandez. Estrada. Ocampo.

As if I'll know which book carries centuries of colonization on its spine just by looking. I forget how our names hide behind other ethnicities. How so often my people are mistaken for what we are not. You only have to hear our names to know.

De Los Santos. De La Cruz. Del Rosario.

As if Catholic syllables could bring us closer to God. As if breathing faith into our family names might bring our families praise. As if keeping our heads down in prayer could keep us safe. As if kneeling at the feet of a foreign king could save us. Maybe that's why we're always forgetting. How brown we are, how brown we've always been. Til they came to water down our family trees. Shake the branches hard enough and a

Conquistador

might fall out. At the reunion, your Tita boasts about how much *Spanish* blood runs in our veins. As if their blood is what ripens our roots as they grow. We all want sampaguita skin for a reason. We use their words to describe how close we are to their image. In order of preference:

Mestiza. Morena. Negrita.

There is one lonely section for the books of color. African American Studies. Latin American Studies. Asian American Studies. They grouped us together so it's easier to keep track of us. Just like naming us made it easier to keep track of us.

Gutierrez. Aquino. Guevara.

It's been centuries since they left our shores, but we still measure our days in their language.

Anong oras na?

Well, it's half-past King Philip, *a las siyete y medya*, time for evening mass. How can colonization leave you?

Lopez. Mendoza. De Guzman.

When its hands built your houses of worship.
When its tongue defines your time.

Flores. Rivera. Castillo.

When it named you.

Sanchez. Garcia. Reyes.

When it named you.

Philippines.

A sestina for my mother tongue

I teach you my language:
tadhana is the word
for fate. I tell you it is the name of a song,
my favorite one, lifted from lyrics
that don't belong in my mouth
to polish and place on an altar.

I don't know the word for altar,
but I know prayer in my language.
Panalangin swirls languid in my mouth
and never reaches my hands. I know the word
only from memorizing the lyrics
of a Tagalog love song.

                    Sing me into a Filipino song:
                    your *kanta* should conjure an altar
                    overflowing with offerings. Soft lyrics,
                    awitin mo in my language
                    until I become a familiar word
                    that swirls in your strange mouth.

                    Shapeshift the tongue in your mouth
                    until your Tagalog sounds like song,
                    a private *harana* in every word,
                    every sentence a new altar.
                    To honor the music of my language
                    sacrifice your own lyrics.

I teach you my lyrics—
they sound painful in your mouth.
Sakit is what we say in my language
for the way you butcher our song.
On a sterile English altar
tadhana is just a word.

Tandaan is the word
for remember, *alaala ko* in lyrics.
I collect Tagalog for my altar
from the muscle memory of my mouth,
I teach myself my language
from the scraps I gather in song.

You cannot approach the altar without knowing my language.
Your mouth scrapes over every Tagalog word.
When you forget the lyrics, I remember I am a foreign song.

Elegy

"A Filipina nurse was assaulted in New York City after she offered face masks to a couple while riding a subway earlier this week.
Nurse and cultural artist Potri Ranka Manis sustained bruises in different parts of her body and had to be brought to an emergency room following the incident last Aug. 10."
—from the article, "Filipina assaulted while giving face masks in New York subway," published by Philstar *on August 14th, 2021*

How many lives does a Filipino have to save before they are allowed to live? How many times have I said I'm *so sorry for your loss* in the past nine months, how many people have been *sorry for my loss* in the past nine months?

In Filipino there are two words for we:
Tayo and kami. We are precise about this: *we* meaning also you, the one I am speaking to and *we* meaning not-you, meaning the other people are not here right now. There are people who are not here right now.

Of all the nurses who have died of COVID-19, one third of them have been Filipino. We are all passing around the same article today as evidence that our collective grief is real.

Kami, like *we* the people, not you, our colonizers, tayo, like *we*, the people's movement, like we need every person within and beyond the Philippines to defamiliarize themselves with empire.

My body only knows it is a body during the sharp disaster of fresh, ripened grief.

Why are there so many Filipino nurses? I googled it once, even though I already knew the answer. I read articles and the common specter stretching itself through history is exploitation. I send them to my friends—we cannot resist something without first giving it a name.

Is it nationalist of me to want to raze Clark Air Base to the ground? We say empires fall, as if we do not need to rigorously destroy their foundations. As if Subic Bay will one day crumble into the sea, with apologies for having been a prime base for the US military.

Tayo, as in *we*, are grieving—everywhere, all the time, collectively. For generations. Do you get it? Do you get it *now*? Tayo, as in *we*, keep losing people—losing, as in, misplaced. How do you lose a person? Is it because at some point we reunite? Kami as in *we*, not you, are grieving. As in, my family specifically. Kami as in *we*, but *you* saying it to *me* this time, you are grieving too. At least we have each other.

"I mean for us to bend
towards what powers us. I mean

we dance inside ourselves even when we're still."

—Hari Alluri, "Hama at Cavern's Mouth (Major Arcana XVIII:
Holder of Shadows)"

in which we have elemental powers, and all the colonizers die

Cento of "Hama at Cavern's Mouth (Major Arcana XVIII: Holder of Shadows)" by Hari Alluri

I found a way to become.

   a residue of moon,

     a prison designed to render

       the invention of another form of key.

When I say bloodbend,

   I mean moon

     I mean you don't need to speak planets and stars

       to plumb down to cruelty: empire

The catastrophe of breaking,

   to live with surviving the end of my own people

     to bend towards our enemy as puppets

       to bend towards power

They're blood too:

   the hands that would extinct me

     can be rendered useless, can be torqued

       can bend towards the moon, arrested

When I say bloodbend

   I mean the tides, I mean we dance

     I mean ourselves, realized and full

       I mean we don't need to bend.

Pantoum for 2032

After Carlos Bulosan, Eman Lacaba, Mila D. Aguilar, and all my kasamas

"A comrade is as precious
as a rice seedling
fed and nurtured
guarded from pestilence and floods"
—Mila D. Aguilar

This is what joy looks like:
palm to palm, radiant, mga kasama.
Sing like every tomorrow is infinite,
each one of us a river, a rush, a dream.

Palm to palm, radiant, mga kasama
smile wide and drink sunlight.
Each one of us a river, a rush, a dream
unfurling into a monumental sea.

Smile wide and drink sunlight,
mga kasama. We are audacious, steady,
unfurling into a monumental sea.
Our life is a truth we have fought for.

Mga kasama! We are audacious, steady.
If a storm should crescendo, remember:
our life is a truth we have fought for,
there is nothing more precious than you.

If a storm should crescendo, remember:
we are millions enough for the thunder,
and there is nothing more precious than you,
mga kasama, holding hands, unafraid.

We are millions enough for the thunder.
We chant, laugh, and dance in the rain,
mga kasama, holding hands, unafraid:
this is what joy looks like.

Mayari begins the solar eclipse

after Maria Bolaños

what is truth
       when refracted through the eyes of the victor?

they tell of the hardheaded girl who fought the god of war and survived
       because of his mercy

       at least they cast me as a fighter   this much is true

but what if I told you of the blood
spilled, the river I made   in the sun, how the terror
       flooded his bright eyes before   he cut out mine?
                                   a cheap shot
from a man who stared into the twin depths of all the world's water
       and knew he would drown.

           what is gentle about a light so violently dimmed?
what is truth:

       I deal in shadows. I tongue darkness into being. My one-eyed
whisper calls forth the night. I turn my eight phases to the universe, my
cycles reign over tides and time.

       If victory is worship, then see how they wait
                   for my fullness to fill the sky

how they howl   for me.

PEKPEK POWER

My pussy tastes like calamansi juice. Yeah, you heard me. Oh, what
do you know about that citrus? It's what you get when you cross a
kumquat with a mandarin orange, hybrid vigor if you know your
biology, hybrid like me, like mixed babae, they call girls like me
mestiza—but fuck that conquistador colloquialism. Call me calamansi.
You better stay thirsty cos this pussy got the juice. So gwapo, let's
get drunk. My pussy tastes like Ginebra, like old school Tanduay,
like lambanog, yes, that coconut moonshine, like you can't drink
this straight, 'cause my pussy isn't straight. So you're gonna need a
chaser, but good luck trying to catch her, good luck trying to control
her. My pussy is willing to take direction on occasion, ask my pussy
politely and she might call you daddy, but not without defiance,
her compliance is not an accident! My pussy gave you permission!
But you always get so cocky, that's confidence with a hard on, well
my pussy's got a boner to pick with you! My pussy's persuasion is
pansexual. She may permit you to enter at her pleasure, wants to be
satisfied, not merely pacified! My pussy is a piano, and I heard you
know how to play. So are you gonna show off an arpeggio? Make it
loud if that's your forte. My pussy wants to know what kind of music
you'll coax out of these keys, and because my pussy is a poet every
orgasm is poetry in motion. And poetry has the power to heal you,
so hit your hallelujah for this healing energy. Like, yeah, my pussy
can save you, but she doesn't *want* to, my pussy is BUSY right now!
Running an organization, planning a community event, producing
a fucking show! My pussy does not have time to recycle all of your
pain unless you plan to fight for her from city hall all the way to
Capitol Hill. My pussy is a filipina resistance movement—My pussy
is kilusan ng paglaban sa pilipinas, Nieves Fernandez guerilla warfare,
learned how to improvise its own weapons. My pussy *is* a weapon
that they're always trying to legislate, but you should capitulate not

dominate, and you should genuflect for this genital flex, because my pussy has no patience for a partisan pity party. My pussy is Princess Urduja of Pangasinan. My pussy is legendary, my pussy is mythical, magical, mystical, pussy magnetic, magnificent, magnanimous, my pussy doesn't punish, my pussy pardons, my pussy is personification of power. Watch the crown, my pussy is coming for it, she's ready for the throne babe, she's running for it. If you see the king tell him to bow down, 'cause my pussy's here to be the king, and she doesn't fuck around.

"I am more and more convinced that true revolutionaries must perceive the revolution, because of its creative and liberating nature, as an act of love."
—Paulo Freire

"As Jimmy Boggs used to remind us, revolutions are made out of love for people and for place. [...] Love isn't about what we did yesterday; it's about what we do today and tomorrow and the day after."
—Grace Lee Boggs

I: River of Time

after Cori Nakamura Lin

remember when you were human
      your raucous weeping pooling
in the base of your throat, a collar-
      bone valley rivered in your sorrow
when do you weep now? what drought
      keeps you awake tonight?

                  at the base of your throat, a collar
                to remind you, you are human
                      are you awake again tonight
                sorrowful in a valley of bones
                  a raucous drought pooling within
                you, unable to weep now

remember when you were river
      a raucous valley, weeping from your bones
what drought could have stopped you?
      being human keeps you from forgetting
how sorrow pools in the throat first
      how you must not collar it or keep it

                  remember when you were free

Writing Prompt:

Write a blessing for your tired body and your troubled mind. A creed, but you are the sacred thing at its center, real, something that can be held. You are ordinary and that is a revelation—to be the standard instead of the exception. Write like there is nothing to measure your tired body and your troubled mind against.

Everyone is having fun at the party

"I don't wanna wait for my life to be over to let myself feel the way I feel
I don't wanna wait for our lives to be over to love myself however I feel,"
—Jamila Woods, "Lonely"

I can't see shit on this rooftop.
Brooklyn pulses unbothered:
I want out of my head, my nest
of razors throbbing, cutting kisses
into the roof of my skull. I want
a full-body press into this railing,
breath to collect in the slope
of my neck, stretched towards
the edge of anguish, a stable
-izing force to pin me to real
-ity. The party spins with mirth
and liquor, slipping exhales
into palms and collarbones. Lust
for home collects in the corner
of my eyes, who will weep with me?
Who will let their joy dangle
from the tightrope of summer,
who will sweat us out to feel alive?
I take my drinks acrid, I want
to escape my void, the tense gnaw
-ing of my psyche must be tempered.
When I am tired
of smiling, who will love
with me?

she/they

fed-up she/her to enraged she/they pipeline:
because it's inevitable, because it's a meme
which is to say that this whole poem is a morsel
of something so much bigger
than itself it can't be digested without sacrifice
which is to say take a shot every time a poet
says "which is to say" in a poem and pour one out
for every loved one you now talk about in the past tense
she/they because grief gives shape to my body
like nothing else, solders me into a recognizable outline
for all my hollow, all my they (she) and her (them), all my
unfinished, which is to say that poets are so good
at transfiguration a poem that begins with an internet joke
turns into something else entirely like the girl that lives
in my clenched jaw and the grooves in my palms
is spiraling beyond comprehension
because it's inescapable, because it's a one-liner
my pronouns are (constantly repressing rage)
she/her clinging to sharp edges my pronouns
are (irreparably expansive) they, they, they holding
hands in the Botanic Gardens, they running
towards the Lake in winter so she'll remember
the biting clarity of aliveness in her lungs, they
crying on the Red Line swaddled in her
warmest coat: she/here against all burdens
they/when all the skin is shed which is to say this
is an offering to a future me/I'm
no longer waiting for permission

A short blessing for my long list of perceived flaws

Hail to the short, the stout, the teapot body of you
The soft dough of your flesh and how warm it keeps you
Hail still to the grace of a round jaw, the sharpest edge of you is on the
inside, and blessed be to the mind that never stops running
Hail to the attention and the never ending stumble, to the razor of your
concentration when it comes, hail still to the collapse when it goes
Hail to the stubborn force of you, yet alive, yet.

self-keeping

which one of you   will press   their gentle   finger   s into my clavicles

and tell me   who i belong to? what   small rage   will grip   inward

and   tighten   around my language

i am only   human,only   a mistake repairing

itself through trials   and so many   errors   so many   mirrors

i am only   a refraction   of someone   else's curses   which one of you

will grab   the heft   of my calf and drag   me   to the ending?

i   cling   to

my   small   rage

i   tighten   my fist, finally

i   swing

Kamayan

I am not an appetizer
They did not plate my bones as a palate cleanser
Or make a tasting menu of my skin
They built my body to endure
Packed my thighs with provisions to get us through the winter
Enough meat in my haunches to feed a nation
When I part my legs parched throats come to imbibe
I am a fountain, a flood, a feast

My body is the loudest despedida in the barangay
They built my body for revelry
Piled me high on banana leaves
Steam rising from my spice-drenched skin
Shoulders soaked in coconut cream
At my table everybody eats
Dig in with your bare hands

My body was made for celebration
For union and reunion
A rebellious toast for every occasion
My mouth is a cup that runs over
My body is meant to overflow
I am dripping out of your hands when your reach for me

I am the storm, the monsoon, the rainfall that quenches the rice field
I am the ripest fruit on the branch
I am an orchard alive with color
Ready for harvest, ready to be picked
Softest of flesh
handle this body with care

Blessing the rice god statue in the full moon

I've come to hate them, the swords:
they appear, these forlorn figures
with blades in their backs,
the blindfolds don't help.

Always they are underneath,
behind, crossing
the tarot card that Gericault says represents me.
In other words, my brain is a box of knives:

I have to draw them out somehow.
I forget what else was in the reading—maybe
the Empress, or the World,
—something about friendship, abundance,

something that calls to mind how it feels
to sit on a blanket in the park
under the full moon,
me and Samer and Gericault,

shivering, cos our gay asses didn't think
to bring coats, huddled around a red
pillar candle, red like the stripes in this blanket
I bought on a whim at Seafood City,

talking about loss, and what it's like to be queer
and how much we want to live, and live, and live and move beyond
all that we have been taught.

We dig our palms into the grass
through the blanket, damp with the essence
of what the day left for us to touch,
I touch the smooth forehead

of the rice god, the heat
of the oven still lingering within the clay
I ask my brain, do you see this shit?
the way Gericault flips

her hair over her shoulder when she speaks,
the way Samer looks when he smiles, beard lined up, the moon
giving light to just enough
of our faces so I can fill the rest in from love.

Last rites

I shook all the linens loose / told all the ghosts to spend the night /
I emptied my house of all the baggage / got my rocks off at the dive
bar / put rocks in my pockets beach-side / I dove into the sea with
the spirits / and had a dance party in the ocean's basement / all this
wonder uncontained / for my last performance / you are all cordially
invited to take a roll / a role / take a load off / take your time /
sweet / take your sweet time in this tide pool / look! the rocks and
the fishes / look! I summoned all the monsters / so we can scratch
them behind the ears / I moved my furniture to give the house more
space / for more of us tumbled on the floor / with clouds with the
blanket of the sky / I unbuttoned the rift between this world and the
next and / I will boldly go / where I have returned so many times
before

II: River of Time

after Tori Ntxoo Hong and Cori Nakamura Lin

Time—like water—changes form but cannot be stopped.
   The pulse of fate drapes us together across universes,
      like water threading through the pores between timelines.
         In every universe I river my way to you, even when my soul
         changes form. A whirlpool in one world, a glass pond in parallel,
      an undulation of possibility we reach for in our own reality *but cannot*
control. All our fates are streaming into an endless gully, who will we *be*
      at the bottom of our shared dreaming, when we have *stopped*
         our undivided aching, pain pooling, losing *time like water?*
         Remember how endless tides erode the rocks they heave against,
            how water *changes form* to freeze apart stones, inevitable.
         In every timeline I choose to be the river that ravines every
            mountain it meets, *but cannot* become ocean without you. In every timeline
we choose to be raindrops, pulsing fates, a monsoon that won't *be stopped.*
Love—like water—changes form but cannot be stopped.

Villanelle for the Water We Swim In

there are so many different words for blue:
azure, turquoise, teal, navy, aquamarine—
when will I return to the ocean?

where will I find words to describe such a loss
of heartspace, of past and future and all between—
there are so many different words for blue.

My small life stretches itself across
borders, and time zones, and screens—
when will I return to the ocean?

I ache for memories, for islands to cross,
the remembrance of something blessed and green—
there are so many different words for blue

how many tender words can I say without cost?
what do we sacrifice to oil this machine?
when will I return to the ocean?

in the belly of the beast I am wary of my thoughts
I dream of water, of something that is still clean.
there are so many different words for blue—
when will I return to the ocean?

An affirmation

for the Asian women in my life, may we one day be free

We look up at the sky and see blue; uninterrupted
and no one tells us we need to step out of the sun
our skin a cloudless glow, we stretch
into our bodies, our wrinkled, our dimpled, our angled, our soft
bodies, our interlaced hands, all of us expanding, unbordered
we nourish ourselves with gusto, we guffaw, we gossip
over the steady thud of mortar and pestle
grinding secret out of spice
our information trade keeps the community safe
we stay safe, we smile for ourselves, a constellation of faces
that can't be lost in shame or shadowed in expectations
our hurricane spirits tear down pedestals
and build altars to ourselves, we hallow
our own bones and together break curse
upon curse upon curse we begin anew
we belong here, and everywhere
we plant our roots in a sky we don't have to hold up
we are all free. we are all, we are, we
we are alive. are alive. alive.

Notes
&
Acknowledgements

Publisher's Note

The Filipino and Tagalog phrases found throughout the collection are translated into English in the following Translation Index. We translate these phrases into English for inclusivity purposes in respect to our non-Filipino and -Tagalog speaking readers.

We are aware of the compromise we make in order to make this art more accessible to a wider audience. In translating these phrases, we participate in a global market that continues to be dictated by Western- and English-supremacist practices. We are also aware that these simple, direct translations of words fall short in communicating their cultural weight and meaning.

We acknowledge the history of translating devices used violently as tools of white gaze revisionism, for the cultural erasure and othering of non-Western, Global South, and diaspora art. This includes the related practice in the United States publishing industry of italicizing words from non-English languages. Our current policy is not to italicize these words unless the poem calls for it.

As cultural discourse, translation methods, and language resources evolve with the times, so may our formatting and translating practices at Sampaguita Press. It is our dream and goal to be able to have our titles commercially available and translated into different languages other than English, for greater language and literary equity.

Translation Index

What Happened in 2020, an inventory of self

"nasaan ang sala? kahit saan kase digital!" – where is the salon? wherever because it's digital!

"Ate" – Older sister

Half-Past King Philip

"De Los Santos. De La Cruz. Del Rosario." – Spanish last names with religious origins. Literally: of the saints, of the cross, and of the rosary.

"Conquistador" – a rotten colonizer

"Mestiza. Morena. Negrita." – words used by Spaniards in colonial Philippines to rank people's skin tone, with an overwhelmingly obvious preference for Mestiza, meaning a light skinned Spanish and Filipino mixed person.

"Anong oras na?" – what time is it?

"a las siyete y medya" – it's seven-thirty

A sestina for my mother tongue

The Filipino and Tagalog words in this poem are italicized intentionally, and in this poem only.

"tadhana" – fate, destiny. A song by Up Dharma Down.

"panalangin" – prayer. A song by APO Hiking Society.

"awitin mo" – you sing. One half of the refrain, "Awitin mo at isasayaw ko," from the song by VST & Co.

"harana" – serenade. A song by Parokya Ni Edgar.

"tandaan" – remember.

"alaala ko" – I remember.

Pantoum for 2032

"mga kasama" – comrades. "Kasama" may also be translated as companion, partner, etc., but in this poem, "kasama" is being used explicitly because of its political connotations in the past and present.

PEKPEK POWER

"babae" – woman/girl

"mestiza" – a mixed White/Filipino person

"lambanog" – a type of coconut spirit in the Philippines, moonshine if you will

"kilusan ng paglaban sa pilipinas" – Philippine resistance movement

Author's Notes

Blessing the Rice God Statue in the Full Moon was first published in *Marías At Sampaguitas* Issue 3, "Binyag/Baptism" in 2021.

Pantoum for 2032 and *A sestina for my mother tongue* were first published in *Marías At Sampaguitas* Issue 2, "Mahal: Who We Are, What It Cost Us, and How We Love" in 2021.

An affirmation won first place in an online poetry contest by *Marías At Sampaguitas* on April 2021. It was originally written in March 2021 for a performance at a community vigil in Chicago honoring the victims of the Atlanta spa mass shooting.

in which we have elemental powers, and all the colonizers die, is a cento using only lines from Hari Alluri's poem *Hama: At Cavern's Mouth*, first published by *Marías At Sampaguitas* Issue 2, "Mahal: Who We Are, What It Cost Us, and How We Love" in 2021.

self-keeping, I: River of Time, II: River of Time are part of an ongoing collaborative art project between me and Cori Nakamura Lin, a visual art and poetry exchange where one artist's work inspires the other to respond, which then becomes a prompt and so on.

Reading Audre Lorde in the kitchen, 3 days before you decided to leave me contains the quote "Men who are afraid to feel must keep women around to do their feeling for them while dismissing us for the same supposedly 'inferior' capacity to feel deeply," from Audre Lorde's essay "Man child: A Black Lesbian Feminist's Response."

Elegy was written during a generative workshop with Kaveh Akbar, partly in response to reading *Fourth Person Singular* by Nuar Alsadir, and in response to workshop discussions on "defamiliarization."

my student asks me what to bring to the protest was written after attending a protest in remembrance of Adam Toledo, a 13 year old boy who was murdered by Chicago police in March 2021. Adam, like so many other people murdered by the police in Chicago and elsewhere, should be alive today.

Mayari begins the solar eclipse is after Maria Bolaños' incredible poem, "Brighter," from her collection *Sana*, published by Sampaguita Press in 2022. It draws from the folktale of how Mayari became the goddess of the moon after a fight with her brother, Apolaki, god of the sun. After the death of their father, Apolaki fought his sister because he wanted to rule all by himself. Their violent battle did not end until Apolaki blinded Mayari in one eye, and apparently realized that fighting over the throne was ridiculous. Supposedly the reason the moon does not shine as brightly as the sun is due to the fact that Mayari only has one eye. And to that I say: well whose fucking fault is that?!

STOP TELLING ME POLICE WILL KEEP US SAFE honors my FMA community. FMA, or Freedom.Movement.Alignment aka Filipino Martial Arts is an offering from my teacher and friend, Crystle Diño. The poem is grounded in the many summer evenings we spent in Ping Tom and elsewhere in Chicago where we learned how to inhabit our bodies, how to fight for ourselves.

Pantoum for 2032 contains a remixing of the following stanza from Carlos Bulosan's poem, "If You Want To Know What We Are,"

> We are multitudes the world over, millions everywhere;
> in violent factories, sordid tenements, crowded cities;
> in skies and seas and rivers, in lands everywhere;
> our number increase as the wide world revolves
> and increases arrogance, hunger, disease and death.

Acknowledgements

Thank you to Maria and Keana for seeing the potential in my work and encouraging me to do this. To them and my editors, Noreen and Kelly, thank you for editing my work with so much care. Thank you all for reading my work and gifting me such intentional, life-affirming, words: beta readers Lillian Rankins, Yvonne Vallejo, Jomari Geronimo, Ellie Lopez, and Mia G. Rios for your time and insights; blurb writers Rachelle Cruz, Jami Nakamura Lin, Taylor Byas, Hari Alluri, Butch Schwarzkopf, Czaerra Galicinao Ucol. Thank you Jason Magabo Perez for your guidance, mentorship, and the incredibly generous foreword you wrote for this book.

Thank you to my IB English Teacher, Charmaine Basel, for nurturing my love of poetry, and a grounding in theater and performance that will stay with me always.

Thank you to the Chicago poets who have left such a mark in my art and in my heart, from our days of slam and more: Mojdeh Stokely, Luis Tubens, Tarnynon Onumonu, Wesley Frazier-Keys, David Wilson, Davon Clark, Caroline Watson, Raych Jackson, Stuti Sharma, Rise Osby, Chandrikah Rukh, Rich Robbins, TJ Medel, AJ Saleh.

To Cori Nakamura Lin, endless thanks for this beautiful cover and these illustrations that capture the soul of my words. To many more years of making art together.

Thank you to the artists whose work makes me feel deeply, and who I return to when I cannot write: Ruby Ibarra, Terisa Siagatonu, Franny Choi, Fatimah Asghar, Jaz Sufi, Kay Ulanday Barrett, Jamila Woods, Jose Olivarez, Hanif Abdurraqib, Barbara Jane Reyes, Monica Ong, Sarah Kay.

I owe so much of my politicization, and what I put into my art, to the work of formations like Malaya Chicago, Anakbayan Chicago, A Just Chi, #COPSOUTCPS, AFIRE Chicago, the Delano Manongs, the Third World Liberation Front; and the work and writings of Carlos Bulosan, Lorena Barros, Grace Lee Boggs, Yuri Kochiyama, Audre Lorde, bell hooks, Mariame Kaba, Kelly Hayes, Benji Hart, and countless other Chicago cultural workers and organizers fighting for our collective liberation.

To everyone who has ever come to a Luya show or workshop, thank you for existing, for traveling from near and far to listen to poetry, for keeping us alive for the past 5 years and many more. Thank you to Jofred Estilo, Stephanie Soultree Camba, Mergen Monotone, King Marie, Elgin Bokari, Alex Wen, Charmaine Balisalisa and Kielle Relles for believing in my vision and supporting Luya from day one. Thank you to Czaerra and Neil for being our small and mighty team, for trusting me, for being baddies I can always count on. Thank you Josh A and Josh Z for being our #1 on-call audio team. Thank you to the countless other people who have ever helped with set up and take down and given rides and reminded me to eat, Luya isn't Luya without you.

To my Ates and Kuyas, thank you for looking out for me. I love you all: Brandon, Carla, Mark, Ryan, Crystle and Natalia.

To my vibrant, queer af, beautiful group of friends who make me laugh til my face hurts, and who make me feel so lucky to be alive: Ai, Alex C, Alex D, Amanda, Amina, Andre, Annie, Ashna, Caroline, Charmaine (again), Chuey, Cori (again), Czaerra (again), Danielle, Eugenia, Gericault, Gilary, HL, Janessa, Josh (again), Kaya, Kristina, Lena, Love, Mai, Mansi, Nick, Noel H, Pooj, Rain, Ren, Roxy, Saul, Shweta, Stuti (again), Vi.

And long live all our overlapping group chats, but specifically shoutout to the West Coast Chicagoans Support Group for the hottest takes on city politics.

Thank you to Ai (again) for being my biggest fan, for seeing me on the days when I cannot see myself, I love you endlessly.

Thank you to the Ucol family for always welcoming me into your home.

Thank you to all of my Titas and Titos and cousins, even though we are spread out across the world I feel your love and support. Thank you especially to Tita Hene, Tito Benjie, Tita Carmina, Tito Bong, for being my home in this country, for taking care of me in so many ways, for always supporting my work, I love you so much.

To my Grandma and Grandpa, to Tita Georgie and Tito Angelo, to Uncle Mark and Aunt Sarah: thank you for welcoming me into the family with open arms, and for seeing the little bookworm I was and encouraging my love of reading.

To my parents and siblings, thank you. Mum, Ben, Sophia - I love you forever and I miss you terribly.

Thank you to my Lola and Lolo, may they rest in peace.

Lastly, thank you to my students Mary, Meron, Feker, Meghana, Safia, Miles, Aila, Sinan, Preston, Sophie and all the young people I have been fortunate enough to organize with. You remind me that our movements should be full of joy and laughter too.

About the Author

Christian Aldana's poetry is a safe space for wicked and sinister femmes who hate imperialism. They are a queer, Filipinx, artist, educator and community organizer based in Chicago. Though she has a soft spot for the Midwest, part of her will always be in South East Asia (Cebu and Saigon) where she grew up.

She is the founder and Creative Director of Luya, a poetry organization that centers the stories and experiences of people of color. Alongside their comrades at The Digital Sala, Christian is dreaming up alternative visions of what radically flexible, community-centered, revolutionary writing spaces can be.

Their poetry has been published by or is forthcoming in the *Chicago Reader*, *Injustice Watch*, *Marías At Sampaguitas*, *The Capilano Review*, and Locked Horn Press. Their performances have been featured at the Poetry Foundation, the Art Institute of Chicago, the Stony Island Arts Bank, Young Chicago Authors, on NPR's Worldview, and more.

When they're not writing poems you can find them in deep discussion about dystopian sci fi, cooking in their pjs, and trying to throw off the tether of scheduled time.

About the Artist

Cori Nakamura Lin (she/her) is a Japanese//Taiwanese-American illustrator and artist specializing in culture-centered storytelling and radical information sharing.

Her work has been published in the *LA Times*, *Eater Chicago*, WBEZ Chicago, PBS Learning Media, and has been featured on the History Channel. She recently illustrated her sister Jami Nakamura Lin's memoir-in-essays, *The Night Parade*, forthcoming in 2023 from Mariner Books/HarperCollins.

Her art roots Asian American folks in collective struggle, by visualizing marginalized narratives and illuminating concepts of abolition, community care and generational curse-breaking. By pushing us to imagine future(s) beyond this current dimension, Cori makes art that fuels action.

www.corilin.co | www.onibaba.studio

Land Acknowledgement

This book was written on Ojibwe, Odawa and Potawatomi lands and produced on Ohlone and Tongva lands.

The staff at Sampaguita Press acknowledge we are settlers on the stolen sacred lands of these Peoples. We remember their connection to these regions and give thanks for the opportunity to live, teach, and learn in their traditional homelands. May we create connections with them, and may we learn Indigenous protocols to become honorable stewards of the land.

We encourage you, Reader, to:

• Amplify the voices of Indigenous people leading grassroots change movements
• Donate your time and money to Indigenous-led organizations
• Politically support the Land Back Movement

In line with these encouragements, Sampaguita Press supports Indigenous art and donates a portion of Press funds raised to Indigenous-led organizations.

In reflecting on our own lives and remembering our family histories, we must remember the legacies of colonialism that we have benefitted from and continue to benefit from as settler-colonialists.

From Palestine to the Philippines, none of us are free until all of us are free.

About Sampaguita Press

Sampaguita Press is an independent micropress publishing house based in San Jose, California. We publish works by and for artists of color. We acknowledge the intersections of identity and support the LGBTQIA+ folk/x in communities of color as well.

Sampaguita Press was founded in 2021 by poets and creatives who wanted to create a space and platform for ourselves, our peers, and other fellow voices who are underrepresented in mainstream publishing.

We strive to inspire progressive change. We acknowledge that change is made with solidarity. We honor and nurture the relationships between our fellow communities. We especially seek works that broaden perspectives and foster understanding.

We believe in racial and social equity. We acknowledge that Western literature and publishing are still overwhelmingly white spaces, and we are committed to amplifying underrepresented voices by providing attention and care to artists who may not have access to traditional publishing spaces.

We are an intersectionally feminist & womanist, inclusive press. We prioritize artists of color of all genders. We discourage hegemonic narratives; hierarchical structures; and supremacist, assimilationist, and normative messaging.

We are a safe literary & linguistic space, and we welcome chapbook submissions in non-English languages.

We support Indigenous rights and sovereignty over the land known as the United States. Our support goes out to the Indigenous groups everywhere in the world who have been harmed, silenced, and displaced. We encourage our readers to learn about and support Indigenous Peoples.